John McNab Currier

Song of Hubbardton Raid

John McNab Currier

Song of Hubbardton Raid

ISBN/EAN: 9783337181574

Printed in Europe, USA, Canada, Australia, Japan

Cover: Foto ©Thomas Meinert / pixelio.de

More available books at **www.hansebooks.com**

SONG OF HUBBARDTON RAID,

DELIVERED ON

The 50 (—1)th Anniversary

OF THE

Raid of the Citizens

OF

HUBBARDTON, VERMONT,

ON

CASTLETON MEDICAL COLLEGE,

HELD AT THE RESIDENCE OF J. SANFORD, M. D.,
CASTLETON, VT., NOVEMBER 29, 1879,

By JOHN M. CURRIER, M. D.

---

*Three hundred copies printed for the members of the Castleton
Medical and Surgical Clinic, for private distribution.
Castleton, Vt., January, 1880.*

PREFACE.

At the annual meeting of the Rutland County Medical and Surgical Society, held at the Otter Creek House in Pittsford, July 9, 1879, Dr. James Sanford of Castleton delivered an able and interesting address, entitled, " Reminiscences of Castleton Medical College," in which he referred to the raid of the citizens of Hubbardton on Castleton Medical College to recover the body of Mrs. Penfield Churchill, which had been stolen from the graveyard in Hubbardton. The society voted unanimously to have it printed in the *Rutland Herald & Globe.* Many of the old students who had attended this once famous institution read the address, and some of them at once challenged the doctor's date of the raid, and wrote to him accord-ingly. On looking into the matter a little closer no one could be found who was absolutely sure his date was right, or at least there was such dis-crepancy of opinions that the doctor did not know on whom to rely. This uncertainty continued until the next regular meeting of the Rutland County Medical and Surgical Society, which was held in Castleton, October 9, 1879. Several toasts were offered and responded to· at the dinner table by various members. "The extinct Medical Colleges of the State" was responded to by Dr. Sanford in a short and humorous speech, in which he again alluded to the Hubbardton Raid, and proposed, as Dr. Currier was interested in all antiquarian matters, to give him one silver "Buzzard" dollar if he would find out the exact date of the raid.

Soon after this meeting Dr. Currier found several

copies of a newspaper printed in Castleton in 1830, giving the true date of the transaction, and thus setting the matter at rest. The following correspondence then took place:

CASTLETON, VERMONT, Oct. 14, 1879.

JAMES SANFORD, M. D.:

Dear Doctor—I have got the exact date of the exhumation of the body of Mrs. Penfield Churchill by the Castleton medical students, also the dates of the attending circumstances. You must be owing me a "Buzzard" dollar about this time,—oysters are legal tender.

Very respectfully,
JOHN M. CURRIER.

P. S. Let us know when the oysters are done and we will go over.

J. N. NORTHROP,
H. A. HAWLEY,
J. E. METCALF.

CASTLETON, VT., Oct. 14, 1879.

Drs. CURRIER, NORTHROP, HAWLEY AND METCALF:

Dear Sirs—I am profoundly thankful for your polite note of to-day, which informs me of your great achievement in the antiquarian matter of

Hubbardton and Castleton. I am also thankful for the consideration you have shown me in giving me an opportunity for an honorable discharge short of the *hard currency.* I will at some future time give an oyster supper to the members of the Castleton Medical and Surgical Clinic. and deem it a pleasure to do so.

I remain, gentlemen, yours with the greatest esteem,
JAMES SANFORD.

Dr. Sanford gave an oyster supper on November 29, 1879, just forty-nine years after the memorable event transpired. It is due him to say that it was not his design to celebrate the anniversary of such a tragedy, but it being so near the time he thought his guests might be a little more inspired with the history of the event.

The following persons were present: Dr. and Mrs. J. N. Northrop; Dr. and Mrs. J. E. Metcalf; Dr. and Mrs. John M. Currier; Mr. and Mrs. Franklin Sanford; Mr. Carlos Sanford; Mr. and Mrs. L. W. Preston; Mrs. Mary Whitlock; Mr.

and Mrs. Luther Fennel, and daughter, Miss Minnie J. Fennel; Mr. B. F. Adams, last secretary of the board of trustees of Castleton Medical College; Mr. B. W. Burt, thirty years correspondent of the *Rutland Herald*, and his daughter, Miss Frankie S. Burt; and Mr. W. C. Guernsey.

After an hour spent in social intercourse the company repaired to the dining room where a supper was served in the most elegant style,—a great honor to Dr. and Mrs. Sanford.

After supper the origin of the entertainment was explained to the company; a history of the Hubbardton Raid was briefly related; and a letter was read from Dr. H. A. Hawley expressing regrets that he could not be present. Dr. Currier then read a poem, entitled "Song of Hubbardton Raid," written in the style of "Hiawatha," giving a full account of the transaction.

At a meeting of the Castleton Medical and Surgical Clinic, held at the residence of Dr. J. N. Northrop, December 15, 1879, Dr. J. E. Metcalf introduced the following resolution, which was unanimously adopted:

Resolved,—That it is the earnest request of the members of this Clinic that Dr. Currier furnish a copy of his poem, entitled "Song of Hubbardton Raid," for publication in pamphlet form.

SONG OF HUBBARDTON RAID.

***

Delivered at an oyster supper given by Dr. and Mrs. Sanford to the members of the Castleton Medical and Surgical Clinic, on the evening of November 29, 1879.

***

BY JOHN M. CURRIER, M. D.

***

Should you ask me whence all these doctors,
With all their pills and physics,
With all their pukes and powders,
Doubly dealing death and destruction,
Attended by their better (poorer) halves,
I should answer, I should tell you:

From their rural wigwams in Castleton,
The land of slates and quarries,
Quarries of green and purple slates,
Slates that never fade nor tarnish,
To celebrate the Hubbardton Raid,
Raid of citizens on Castleton Medical College,
Long ago in the early history of our town,
Fifty years ago. They have come to celebrate,
And to get one *good, square meal.*

In this land of slates and quarries,
Quarries that furnished slates of various hues,
Was the seat of medical learning
Where the youthful Esculapians learned to bleed,
To bleed from the arm with a lancet,
To bleed from their patients' pockets,
Pockets filled with *honest* silver dollars,
Here in this modern rural Athens,
In this quiet Green Mountain hamlet,

Came these aspiring youths,
Youths with handsome faces and fair,
To learn the structure of the human body, ˄
To learn how the parts were put together;
To flirt with the seminary maidens.

They came to hear the wise ones,
Wise ones with learning and dignity,
Talk of the muscles, the bones and nerves, ·
Tell their origins and insertions,
Tell their processes, grooves and ridges,
Tell their ramifications and inosculations,
Tell how they cured their patients,
How they dressed wounds, bleeding wounds,
In this town of slates and quarries,
In this town of green and purple slates,
In this quiet Green Mountain hamlet.

When the faded leaves of autumn

Began to rustle in the chilly breezes,
These *studious emetics* gathered in,
Gathered around the lecture amphitheater,
Gathered around the dissecting table,
With knives, and saws, and forceps,
Around dead human frames and bones,
To learn their relations and structure,
In this land of slates and quarries,
Quarries of green and purple slates,
They came to learn anatomy; the muscles :
Serratus posticus superior,
Serratus posticus inferior,
Genio-hyo-glossus, sterno-mastoideus,
These familiar muscles came they to learn:
Extensor secundi internodii,
Extensor communis digitorum,
Extensor proprius policis,
Extensor carpi radialis brevior,
Extensor carpi radialis longior,

And many more of these easy names
Could they learn and remember
In this Green Mountain Athens,
In this land of slates and quarries,
Quarries of green and purple slates,
Slates that never fade nor tarnish.

In this ancient seat of learning,
In this house of dead flesh and bones,
Were set up long rows of tables,
Tables covered with human bodies,
Tables covered with stains of human blood,
Tables unwashed for many years,
In this land of slates and quarries.
Around these tables they dissected,
Dissected with a relish and love,
To learn the structure of the body,
To learn the different diseases,

2   •

In the town of green and purple slates.
Whoever died for miles around,
This numerous and savage class,
This class of savage students,
Was sure to adorn these tables,
Their flesh would feed the students' fire,
In this land of slates and quarries.
The friends would deck the graves,
Deck the mounds with fragrant flowers,
And drop a tear o'er empty coffins,
Coffins rifled of their contents,
In this Green Mountain Athens,
In this town of slates and quarries,
Quarries of green and purple slates,
Slates that never fade nor tarnish.

When the chill winds of November
Were sifting the snow flakes through the branches,
Through the dry branches of the trees,

Along the frozen roadside,
Roadside hubbly and rough,
In the wildwoods of Hubbardtown,
The land of battle, but not of song,
The land of cider and bean porridge,
The land of johnny cake and hominy,
The land of early rose potatoes,
Potatoes of red skins and smooth,
In the year of our Lord and Saviour,
One thousand, eight hundred and thirty,
Of American independence, fifty-four,
Of the year of anti-masonry, five,
A cherished wife was laid in her tomb,
In a tomb deep and narrow,
In the wildwoods of Hubbardton,
In the land of early rose potatoes.
Many were her friends, the whole town,
Who never more expected to view
The remains again on earth;

Sadly the sods were shoveled in,
Shoveled in by the honest sexton,
Shoveled in amidst the flow of tears,
Shoveled in as the friends returned home;
The mound was rounded over,
A mound, high and covered with sods,
In the wildwoods of Hubbardton.
The cunning sexton placed a secret mark
On the grave to mark the repose,
And watched the footsteps of students
From the land of slates and quarries,
From the Green Mountain Athens,
From the land of green and purple slates.

The sexton, when a few days had passed,
Went to the grave of his friend,
The grave covered high with sods,
In the wildwoods of Hubbardton,
The land of johnny cake and hominy,

And discovered his mark disturbed ;
The sods displaced and torn.
Resurrection had commenced
In the wildwoods of Hubbardton,
In the land of cider and bean porridge,
The land of battle, but not of song,
The land of early rose potatoes.!
The sexton spread the story,
Spread the story of resurrection,
Spread it to every household
In the wildwoods of Hubbardton,
The land of battle, but not of song.
The news excited every breast,
Every heart beat with heavy throbs
As the news spread though the forests,
The land of early rose potatoes.
As the news went from door to door,
These rustics started for the graveyard,
Started for the graveyard of their friends,

Graveyard filled with none but friends,
Friends very dear to all in town,
In the land of early rose potatoes.
They came pouring in from all points :
From the east and from the west,
From the north and from the south.
As the sexton shoveled out the sods,
Shoveled the sods from this sacred spot,
In they thronged ; the crowd grew larger ;
As the sexton neared the coffin
The excitement grew stronger.
And the hollow sound grew louder ;
It echoed from the forests
In the wildwoods of Hubbardton,
The land of johnny cake and hominy,
Hominy made from the corn,
From the yellow corn pounded coarse,
From the golden, yellow, shining corn,
In the land of battle, but not of song.

The sexton raised the coffin lid,
Coffin lid made of sugar maple,
Filled with screws, shining and bright,
Raised he this coffin lid of maple.
The coffin was empty ! the body stolen !
The awful fact of resurrection
Fired the wrath of the beholders,
Fired them all to vengeance,
Fired these rustics of the forest,
In the wildwoods of Hubbardton.
Vengeance fell on Green Mountain Athens,
On its rural seat of medical learning,
In the land of slates and quarries,
Quarries of green and purple slates,
Slates that never fade nor tarnish.

A council of war was held from day to day,
In this town of battle, but not of song,
To decide the course their vengeance should take,

The vengeance burning in every breast.
Sunday night their plans were laid,
Plans, deep and strong, for the morrow,
At nine o'clock on Monday morning,
No storms of snow or rain should prevent,
Not one minute later, not one minute sooner,
Should these raiders meet in Athens,
In the land of slates and quarries,
On the twenty-ninth day of November,
To search that ancient seat of learning.

Ere the sunlight lit the tree-tops,
On that memorable Monday morning,
When still the darkness shrouded the forests
In the wildwoods of Hubbardton,
In the land of cider and bean porridge,
Porridge made of large speckled beans,
Porridge thickened with Indian meal,
Meal from the golden, yellow corn,

In the land of early rose potatoes.

Ere the sunlight lit the tree-tops,

Lit the topmost branches of the forests,

These rustic Hubbardtonians collected

Into rank and file for duty ;

All were dressed in long drab overcoats,

Coats reaching down to the malleoli, the ankles,

Coats with several capes about the shoulders,

Capes that shingled-off at the elbows,

Long drab coats with chains and buttons ;

Cowhide boots, stout and thick,

Cowhide boots with heavy soles,

Double soles with two rows of nails,

Soles thirteen inches long, or more,

In the land of johnny cake and hominy.

Each man was armed with a wooden club,

Clubs heavy and strong to defend their honor,

Clubs of beech, and clubs of hickory,

Clubs of birch, and sugar maple,

Clubs of ash from the forests,
In the wildwoods of Hubbardton,
The land of early rose potatoes.

Three regiments were formed,
Regiments of one hundred each,
Mustered in this rustic town,
Prepared for battle on its stumpy plains,
And took up its long line of march
To the land of slates and quarries,
To this Green Mountain Athens,
To this ancient seat of learning.
Some rode on horseback,
Some rode in carriages,
Carriages painted green and yellow;
Some rode on foot in cowhide boots,
Cowhide boots with heavy soles.
Through the wildwoods of Hubbardton,
The land of battle, but not of song.

The main army took the military road,
The old military road through the county
Fresh with the footsteps of Ethan Allen
On his way to capture Ticonderoga,
Through the wildwoods of Hubbardton.
The left flank, with its banners flying,
Unfurled to catch the first rays of sunlight,
Took the route of Burgoyne's army
To the land of slates and quarries,
Quarries of green and purple slates,
Slates that never fade nor tarnish.
General Dike, the sheriff, was the leader,
With papers in his pocket to take the town,
This Green Mountain Athens,
This ancient seat of learning.
The right flank with its sturdy leader
Came puffing down the lake road,
With their caps and coat tails flying   [banners,
In the early morning breezes that swelled their

Through the rustic wildwoods of Hubbardton.
Into the ancient town of learning,
This renowned seat of medical lore,
In the land of slates and quarries.

When the bell tolled the hour of nine,
Tolled the hour for students to meet,
In this ancient seat of learning,
In this Green Mountain Athens,
These three mighty, rustic armies
Surrounded Castleton Medical College ;
Formed a line around its walls,
A double row of pickets to make it sure,
And demanded unconditional surrender
Of this ancient seat of learning,
In this land of slates and quarries,
Slates that never fade nor tarnish.
The *Dean* stood in the door and said :
" Whoever enters this building

Must walk over my dead body."
The mighty army stood gaping at his words,
Stood with their mouths wide open,
Around the walls of the college,
Stood these rustic soldiers of Hubbardton,
The land of battle, but not of song,
The land of early rose potatoes,
Their war-clubs dangling by their sides,
They stood amazed at such defiance,
In the land of slates and quarries.

Sheriff Dike then informed the *Dean*
That he had legal papers to make a search
Within the walls of this seat of learning,
In this Green Mountain hamlet,
To find the body of the faithful wife,
To find the remains stolen away,
Stolen from the sacred graveyard

3

In the wildwoods of Hubbardton,
The land of battle, but not of song.
The Dean replied in milder tones
That he could go in as a legal posse,
As an officer having authority,
But never as a military commander,
As the general of such a mighty army
From the land of cider and bean porridge,
From the wildwoods of Hubbardton.
But where was the key, said the Dean ;
The key that unlocks the college door·;
The iron key that turns the bolt
In this ancient seat of learning,
In this Green Mountain Athens,
In this land of slates and quarries !
The cunning Dean, fostering delay,
Sent for his key at home by one
Who was noted for being slow,
While the key was in his pocket,

Safely lodged from armed intruders,
From the land of early rose potatoes.
The busy students inside dissecting,
Dissecting human flesh and bones,
To learn the structure of the human body,
Hearing the outcry of vengeance at the door,
Severed the head from the body,
Out the head from off the corpse,
That was stolen from the graveyard,
From the sacred graveyard in Hubbardton,
The land of battle, but not of song.
The body was secreted behind a board,
A board that was nailed in place,
A nook in this ancient seat of learning,
In this Green Mountain hamlet,
In the land of slates and quarries,
Slates that never fade nor tarnish.

A student of great composure,
Always self-possessed and firm,
Took the head under his cloak,
Under his elegant cloak of beaver,
Walked through the crowd unsuspected,
Through this crowd of rustic soldiers,   ·
Through this crowd of Hubbardtonians,
And hid away his prize in a hay loft,
In this modern Green Mountain Athens,
In the land of slates and quarries.

The doors were opened, the search began,
The horrors of the dissecting room appeared,
Skeletons hung up around the walls,
Hung up with hempen strings,
Partly dissected bodies met their eyes everywhere,
Staring faces without any eyes,
Limbs half dissected, on the floor,
In the chairs and on the tables,

Mingled with the students' dinner pails,

Such ghastly mixtures never before seen

By these rustic citizen-soldiers,

In the land of johnny cake and hominy,

In the wildwoods of Hubbardton.

Such ghastly sights! such human merchandise!

Long rows of tables of mangled remains!

Dirt and filth, saws, knives and forceps,

Bones, muscles, and parts of flesh, lay in piles,

In this ancient seat of learning,

In this land of slates and quarries.

No learned anatomist in any college

Could tell a youth from an adult;

Could tell a Negro from a Yankee;

Could tell a Squaw from a Scotchman;

Out of such a motly mess of human debris.

So the sheriff told the husband,

This husband filled with sadness and sorrow,

From the wildwoods of Hubbardton,

To identify his beloved wife,
The cherished wife of his early years,
The dear companion of the forests
In the land of battle, but not of song.
He groped about among the tables,
Squinted here and there among the subjects,
And picked out one from certain marks
That he could call his wife, under oath ;
And was ready to pack it up and start
For the land of early rose potatoes,
When the professor, learned and wise,
Told him that subject was a burly Negro,
And wore a number fourteen boot,
And never gathered spruce gum in the forests,
In the wildwoods of Hubbardton.

The students offered these raiders
Bones and flesh enough to make a wife
If they would quietly take them and depart

For the stumpy plains of Hubbardton.
This jocose remark provoked their wrath,
And after hours of fruitless search,
They swore they would burn the town
If the stolen body was not produced,
If not brought forth from its lurking place
In this ancient seat of learning,
In this Green Mountain Athens,
In the land of slates and quarries,
In the land of purple and green slates,
Slates that never fade nor tarnish.

The search was renewed by these raiders,
A closer search by these citizen-soldiers,
By these citizen-soldiers in long drab coats,
Coats with shingled-off capes at the elbows,
Stamping round the hall in cowhide boots,
Pegged and nailed by rustic shoemakers,
From the land of early rose potatoes.

A suspicious nail-head revealed the secret,
Told the story of human resurrection,
Disclosed the hiding place of the body,
The body of the wife stolen from the graveyard,
From the sacred graveyard in Hubbardton,
The land of battle, but not of song.
In the students' hurry to conceal the body
A nail—an iron nail, was left undriven.
This suspicious nail-head revealed the secret,
Told the story of human resurrection,
Disclosed the hiding place of the body,
In this Green Mountain Athens,
In this land of slates and quarries,
In this land of medical learning.

They pulled up a board from the floor,
From this ancient seat of learning,
And saw the body of the missing wife,
The headless body of the exhumed woman,

Thrust into a cramped up corner.
These rustic raiders stood horrified
Before this awful spectacle!
This awful deed committed by the students
In this ancient seat of learning,
By the students of Castleton Medical College.
The husband identified the remains,
Could say they were his wife's, under oath,
The body that was stolen from the graveyard,
From the sacred graveyard in Hubbardton,
From the land of battle, but not of song.

By way of compromise with these raiders,
This rustic cavalry from Hubbardton,
The students offered to throw in the head
If they would leave this land in peace,
Leave this ancient seat of learning,
Leave this land of slates and quarries.
They picked up this human merchandise,

This batch of stolen property,
Stolen from the graveyard in Hubbardton ;
Packed it in a box on some straw,
In a box made from the native pine,
Nailed with wrought nails of iron,
Nails made by native blacksmiths,
Native blacksmiths from Hubbardton,
The land of battle, but not of song.
These three mighty armies fell into line,
They formed one grand procession,
They took up their long line of march.
To the wildwoods of Hubbardton,
The land of battle, but not of song,
The land of cider and bean porridge,
The land of johnny cake and hominy,
The land of early rose potatoes.

We have met to-night to commemorate
The forty-ninth anniversary

Of this awful and wicked tragedy ;
To show to all future generations,
To all generations coming after this,
The troubles and trials of medical learning,
The difficulty in getting medical knowledge,
In this ancient seat of learning,
In this once famous Castleton Medical College.
We came to feast on Dr. Sanford's oysters,
Pick the meats from the bivalves,
Peppered as the jest goes round ;
We came to sip the doctor's coffee ;
Coffee—not his pills, pukes and powders—
His coffee, flavored with sugar and cream—
Sugar from the cane, cream from the Jerseys ;
We came to eat his cakes and cookies,
We came to share his happiness ;
And may we long remember the time
We have so pleasantly spent together
At this rural wigwam in Castleton,

The land of slates and quarries,
Quarries that furnish slates of various hues,
Quarries of green and purple slates,
In this Green Mountain hamlet,
In this rural modern Athens,
In this town of slates and quarries,
Slates that never fade nor tarnish.

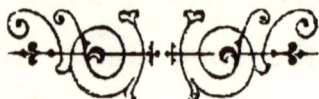